JESUS ISN'T SOFT

JESUS ISN'T SOFT
KNOWING JESUS' AUTHENTIC TOUGHNESS

CHARLIE ARTZ

Book design by eBook Prep
www.ebookprep.com

April 2023
ISBN: 978-1-64457-619-9

Rise UP Publications
644 Shrewsbury Commons Ave
Ste 249
Shrewsbury PA 17361
United States of America
www.riseUPpublications.com
Phone: 866-846-5123

To the Lord God Almighty, who was and is and is to come; to Jesus Messiah, Lion of the Tribe of Judah and the Lamb of God; to Holy Spirit Counselor Helper Intercessor and Spirit of Truth: Blessing and Honor and Glory and Power to You!

To my four beautiful, brilliant, anointed, healed, and hilarious children, Abby, Jake, Olivia, and Hannah: thank you for your endless love, support, presence, care, humor, hard work, strength, faith, and integrity. I have no greater joy than to know that my children walk in the truth.

To Ibukun Blessing Beautiful Overcomer Prophetess WordGirl Dr. O: thank you for your care, support, encouragement, and love, and for being my Person.

To Paster David Payton: thank you for prophesying this book. To Pastor Philip Thornton: thank you for your relentless exposition of Word and Faith and for building big people. To Dr. Philip Derber: thank you for publicly stating this writing needs to be done.

To my Dad, who walks in Glorious Freedom with Jesus: thank you for your legacy of faith and love and for prophesying the call of my life to spread the Gospel when all I cared about was baseball.

But who do you say that I am?

—JESUS CHRIST, MATTHEW 16:15

INTRODUCTION

The *historicity* of Jesus of Nazareth is indisputable. More evidence documents Jesus' walk on the earth than Tiberius Caesar, the Roman political ruler who lived during Jesus' first time on earth.[1]

The *exclusivity* of Jesus the Messiah is firmly established in His own Words:

> *I am the way, the truth, and the life. No one comes to the*
> *Father except through Me.*
>
> — JOHN 14:6 (NIV)

The *eternicity*[2] of Jesus conclusively establishes His status as the Son of God, who was God and was with God from the beginning.[3] When He confronted the religious leaders who walked in unbelief, Jesus declared:

Before Abraham was, I AM

—JOHN 8:58

People tend to limit Jesus based on their personality, needs or likeness. They try to jam Jesus into a mold consistent with what they want Jesus to be, *not who Jesus is*. No reasonable basis in fact or in law (i.e., The Word) justifies that approach.

The Lord God Almighty's plan for this phase of my life is to recruit, equip, train and mobilize spiritual warriors for spiritual battle in the marketplace, the gym, the home and the ballpark to facilitate a personal move of God in people's lives to effectuate local, regional and national revival. The Holy Spirit directed that mission statement in those specific words on November 13, 2022.

This is the first in a series of practical, short, linear and logical books to provide specific spiritual warfare implementation specifications. Dozens of excellent spiritual warfare books exist. Read as many as you can. Most accurately address conceptual spiritual warfare. The revelations discussed below fill the gap between conceptual warfare and specific implementation steps.

This text documents multiple revelations defining the complete nature of Jesus, the Messiah. The number three in the Word of God signifies perfection. Jesus exemplified perfect Love, perfect Truth and perfect Fire. Just as the Father, the Son and the Holy Spirit are separate but one unified Deity, Jesus' Love, Jesus' Truth and Jesus' Fire are separate but unified.

The intended audiences include the following:

- Misinformed people who think Jesus was (or is) soft;
- People of Faith who want to truly know Jesus and the Power of His Resurrection, to walk as Jesus walked, and to internalize Jesus' authentic toughness;
- Lost people who live in unbelief;
- People who reject and blaspheme Jesus so they have a chance to repent;
- People who are incarcerated, literally in a federal or state prison, and figuratively because of spiritual or other addictive bondage;
- Pastors and priests who propagate a soft Jesus to justify their own weakness, unbelief, lack of faith or to advance a political agenda in contradiction of God's unequivocal Word; and
- Spiritual Warriors walking in great Faith who periodically rely on Jesus' authentic toughness solely in the flesh and not in the spirit.

People of Faith are called to love people to the same extraordinary extent that Jesus loved people. People of Faith are called to know, apply and share the Truth. Spiritual Warriors are called to fight wickedness with Fire, using the Sword, which is the Word of God, to walk in great Faith and effectuate Freedom.

INTRODUCTION

1. *Evidence That Demands a Verdict*, Josh McDowell & Sean McDowell, Ph.D.
2. Corporate America manufactures new words all the time. *Eternicity* means the eternal nature of Jesus.
3. John 1:1-2.

CHAPTER 1
KNOW JESUS

The Apostle Paul wrote:

*But what things were gain to me, these I have counted
loss for Christ. Yet indeed I also count all things
loss for the excellence of the knowledge of Christ
Jesus my Lord, for whom I have suffered the loss of
all things, and count them as rubbish, that I may
gain Christ and be found in Him, not having my own
righteousness, which is from the law, but that
which is through faith in Christ, the righteousness
which is from God by faith; that I may know Him
and the power of His resurrection, and the fellowship
of His sufferings, being conformed to His death, if,
by any means, I may attain to the resurrection from
the dead.*

— PHILIPPIANS 3:7-11

The NIV states, *"I want to know Him and the power of His resurrection."* The context seems almost aspirational. It appears as something for which we are to strive. That is true, of course; however, I have turned that into an affirmative confession and prayer: *Jesus, I know you and the power of your resurrection in my life.*

What does that mean in practical terms? If one person wants to know another person, you learn the other person's names, nicknames and preferred names. You listen to the other person. You talk to the other person. You tell the other person your secrets. You ask the other person questions. You listen to the other person's questions asked of you; you learn the other person's attributes.

How is this practically applied? It means we need to know all of Jesus' names. We need to listen to Jesus through His Word. We need to talk to Jesus and explain basic things in our lives, but also have deep conversations that do not include nonsense and selfish desires. We need to tell Jesus our secrets. We can ask any question of Jesus. We need to pay attention to the questions Jesus asked.[1] On a daily basis, we should explore Jesus' Love; Jesus' Truth; and Jesus' Fire.

Jesus' Names include all of the following:

- Wonderful Counselor/Mighty God/Everlasting Father/Prince of Peace – Isaiah 9:6
- Immanuel – Matthew 1:23
- Messiah/Anointed One – Matthew 16:16

- Word – John 1:1
- Life – John 1:4
- Light – John 1:14
- Truth – John 1:14
- One and Only – John 1:14
- Lamb of God – John 1:29, 35
- Son of God – John 1:49
- Son of Man – John 1:51
- Living Water – John 4:10
- Bread of Life – John 6:35, 48
- Light of Life – John 8:12
- I Am – John 8:58
- The Gate – John 10:7
- The Good Shepherd – John 10:14
- The Resurrection and the Life – John 11:25
- The Way, the Truth and the Life – John 14:6
- My Lord and My God – John 20:28
- Prince of Life – Acts 3:15
- Author of Life – Acts 3:16
- Capstone – Acts 4:11
- Salvation – Acts 4:12
- Anointed One – Acts 4:24
- Just One – Acts 7:51
- King of Peace – Hebrews 7:2
- King of Righteousness – Hebrews 7:2
- Surety/Guarantor of New Covenant – Hebrews 7:22
- Interceder – Romans 8:34; Hebrews 7:25
- Mediator – Hebrews 12:24
- Living Stone – 1 Peter 2:4
- Chief Shepherd – 1 Peter 5:4

- Advocate – 1 John 2:1
- Faithful Witness – Revelation 1:5
- Lion of Judah – Revelation 5:5
- Faithful and True – Revelation 19:11-15
- Name Written on Him that no one knew except Himself – Revelation 19:12
- Word of God – Revelation 19:13
- King of Kings – Revelation 19:16
- Lord of Lords – Revelation 19:16
- Alpha and Omega – Revelation 22:13

Practical implementation: Read one or more of these passages every day. When you know Jesus' Names, you will get to know Jesus.

Throughout the Book of Acts, those who believed Jesus proclaimed His Name multiple times. The Book of Acts repeatedly states that the believers referenced the "Name of Jesus" at least 19 times.[2]

---

1. By my count, Jesus asked over 100 questions as documented in Matthew, Mark, Luke and John. This will be the subject of another text.
2. This will be explained in detail in the upcoming Book entitled *ActX Warriors*.

CHAPTER 2
JESUS FIRE

Knowing Jesus' authentic toughness compels understanding, not just in your head but all the way into your soul and spirit, under what circumstances Jesus demonstrated His perfectly unified Love, Truth and Fire. Jesus' Fire arguably was not brought against any individual human being. On the contrary, Jesus' Fire manifested against all of the following:

- Hypocrisy
- Useless Religious Traditions
- Spiritual Blindness
- Superficiality
- Neglect of Justice, Mercy and Faith
- Nullification of the Word by Spiritually Worthless Bureaucratic Rules and Regulations
- Wickedness
- Unbelief
- Oppression
- Tyranny

The Spiritual Warrior is called to spiritual battle. The Spiritual Warrior must be led by the Spirit, not by the flesh. Dropping into the flesh results in fighting with other humans. Fighting against other human beings, for whom Jesus died, means we are no different than the world. The only way we can walk as Jesus walked is to live *in Him* and *know Him*.[1]

FIRE

Knowing Jesus' authentic toughness, and eradicating a blasphemous soft perception of Jesus, begins with **Fire**. Jesus said:

> *I came to send fire on the earth and how I wish it were already kindled! But I have a baptism to be baptized with, and how distressed I am until it is accomplished!*

> — LUKE 12:49

John the Baptist prophesied this very characteristic in the context of Pharisees and Sadducees coming to his baptism. Matthew records John the Baptist stating:

> *And even now the ax is laid to the root of the trees. Therefore, every tree which does not bear good fruit is cut down and thrown into the <u>fire</u>. I indeed baptize you with water unto repentance, but He who is coming after me is mightier than I, whose sandals I am not worthy to carry. He will baptize you with the <u>Holy</u>*

*Spirit and fire. His winnowing fan is in His hand,
and He will thoroughly clean out His threshing floor,
and gather His wheat into the barn; but He will
burn up the chaff with unquenchable fire.*

— MATTHEW 3:10-12

Jesus taught that the Kingdom of Heaven is like a man who sowed good seed in his field. When the man slept, the enemy came in and sowed tares among the wheat and went his way. In response to the disciples' request to explain the parable of the tares of the field, Jesus said:

*He who sows the good seed is the Son of Man. The field
    is the world, the good seed are the sons of the king-
    dom, but the tares are the sons of the wicked one. The
    enemy who sowed them is the devil, the harvest is the
    end of the age, and the reapers are the angels. There-
    fore, as the tares are gathered and burned in the fire,
    so it will be at the end of this age. The Son of Man
    will send out His angels, and they will gather out of
    His kingdom all things that offend, and those who
    practice lawlessness, and will cast them into the
    furnace of fire. There will be wailing and gnashing
    of teeth.
The angels will come forth, separate the wicked from
    among the just, and cast them into the furnace of fire.*

— MATTHEW 13:37-42, 49-50

When speaking of the coming Kingdom of God, Jesus said:

> *It was the same in the days of Lot. People were eating and drinking, buying and selling, planting and building. But the day Lot left Sodom, <u>fire</u> and sulfur rained down from Heaven and <u>destroyed them all</u>. It will be <u>just like this on the day the Son of Man is revealed</u>.*
>
> — LUKE 17:28-30 (NIV)

The context demonstrates Jesus was explaining it will be just like that in the days of the Son of Man as it was in the days of Noah. Wickedness reigned. Evil was ubiquitous. Jesus did not and will not tolerate[2] wickedness. Neither should Spiritual Warriors.

John's Revelation on the Island of Patmos describes the Resurrected Jesus as follows:

> *His head and hair were white like wool, as white as snow, and his eyes were <u>like blazing fire</u>. His feet were like bronze glowing in a furnace, and his voice was like the sound of rushing waters. In his right hand, he held seven stars, and out of his mouth came a <u>sharp, double-edged sword</u>. His face was like the sun shining in all its brilliance.*
>
> — REVELATION 1:14-16 (NKJV,NIV)

The Fire in the Resurrected Jesus' eyes is further described in Jesus' directive to John regarding the Church in Thyatira:

> *These are the words of the Son of God, whose eyes are like <u>blazing fire</u>.*

> — REVELATION 2:18 (NIV)

This fire was directed against the Church's tolerance of Jezebel. Jesus has no tolerance for misleading teaching, sexual immorality and eating food sacrificed to idols. Unless they repent, they will suffer intensely. Jesus searches hearts and minds and will repay according to evil deeds. Spiritual Warriors are called to pray and act against wickedness and encourage repentance.

A word of caution from personal experience:

> *Don't bring Jesus' Fire unless you have identified, repented from, and surrendered all forms of sin and wickedness.*

Jesus' second coming will be on a victorious White Horse:

> *I saw heaven standing open and there before me was a white horse, whose rider is called Faithful and True. With justice he judges and wages war. His eyes are like <u>blazing fire</u>, and on his head are many crowns. He has a name written on him that no one knows but he himself. He is dressed in a robe*

23

dipped in blood, and his name is the Word of God.
The armies of heaven were following him, riding
on white horses and dressed in fine linen, white and
clean. Coming out of his mouth is a <u>sharp sword</u>
with which to strike down the nations. "He will
rule them with an iron scepter." He treads the
winepress of the fury of the wrath of God
Almighty. On his robe and on his thigh he has this
name written: KING OF KINGS AND LORD
OF LORDS.[3]

— REVELATION 19:11-16 (NIV)

After Jesus' thousand years' reign on earth, and before the New Jerusalem arrives, Satan will be released from his prison and will deceive the nations. They will attempt to war one last time, but it will be unsuccessful:

But fire came down from heaven and devoured them.[4]

— REVELATION 20:9

Peter must have seen the same thing. Peter foretold the last days, described the flood that initially destroyed wickedness, and contrasted it with Jesus' second coming:

By the same word the present heavens and earth are
reserved for <u>fire</u>, being kept for the day of judgment
and destruction of the ungodly.
But the day of the Lord will come like a thief. The
heavens will disappear with a roar; the elements will

*be destroyed by fire, and the earth and everything done
in it will be laid bare.*

*That day will bring about the destruction of the heavens
by fire, and the elements will melt in the heat. But in
keeping with his promise we are looking forward to a
new heaven and a new earth, where righteousness
dwells.*

— 2 PETER 3:7, 11-13 (NIV)

Paul wrote about God's just judgment:

*God is just: He will pay back trouble to those who trouble
you and give relief to you who are troubled, and to us
as well. This will happen when the Lord Jesus is
revealed from heaven in blazing fire with his powerful
angels.*

— 2 THESSALONIANS 1:6-7 (NIV)

Understanding Fire in natural terms helps to visualize
Jesus' Fire:

Fire is the visible effect of the process of combustion—a special type of chemical reaction. It occurs
between oxygen in the air and some sort of fuel. The
products from the chemical reaction are completely
different from the starting material.

The fuel must be heated to its ignition temperature
for combustion to occur. The reaction will keep going

as long as there is enough heat, fuel and oxygen. This is known as the fire triangle.[5]

The oxygen, fuel and heat fire triangle may be symbolic of triplicate perfection. In the fullness of time, and when God's creative power (fuel), the Holy Spirit (oxygen) and Jesus' "high heat" are combined, there will be a combustion on the earth. Combustion results in a flame that is very fast, which is known as burning.[6] Knowing Jesus' authentic toughness means knowing that He is going to bring Fire. His unparalleled love will allow every one of us to repent. But the Word promises that "each person will be judged according to what he had done."[7] Jesus' Fire is reserved for unrepentant sinning and wickedness. There is nothing soft about Jesus' Fire.

SWORD

Jesus' authentic toughness confirms He is also the **Sword**. He shreds all of the devil's evil and wickedness with the **Sword**. Multiple scriptural passages confirm this:

> *Out of his mouth came a sharp <u>double-edged sword</u>.*[8]
> *These are the words of him who has the <u>sharp, double-edged sword</u>. Repent therefore! Otherwise, I will soon come to you and will fight against them with the <u>sword</u> of my mouth.*
>
> — REVELATION 2:12, 16 (NIV)

The first reference is the manifestation of the Resurrected Jesus. The second is His call to repentance to the Church in Pergamum that held to the teaching of Balaam, which, again, involved eating food sacrificed to idols and committing sexual immorality.

At His second coming, when he appears on the White Horse:

> Out of his mouth comes a <u>sharp sword</u> with which to strike down the nations.
> The two of them [the beast and the false prophet] were thrown alive into the fiery lake of burning sulfur. The rest of them [those who took the mark, and followed the beast and the false prophet] were <u>killed with the sword</u> that came out of the mouth of the rider on the horse, and all the birds gorged themselves on their flesh.
>
> — REVELATION 19:15, 21 (NIV)

We see clearly Jesus' Sword both saves and kills. Jesus is our only path to salvation. Jesus will not tolerate blasphemy.

When Jesus called His twelve disciples, He gave them power over unclean spirits, to cast out unclean spirits and to heal all kinds of sickness and all kinds of disease. Jesus said:

> *Do not think that I came to bring peace on earth. I did not*
> *come to bring peace but a <u>sword</u>.*

— MATTHEW 10:34

I can hear it now. *Jesus did not say that. You took it out of context.* Oh yes, He did. And oh, no, I didn't. In fact, as long as sin prevails in the earth, there will not be peace on earth. The fantastic Christmas phrase, "On earth, peace, good will toward men",[9] means people who come to Faith in Jesus are not at war with God. Jesus said, "In the world you will have tribulation, but in Me you will have peace. Be of good cheer, I have overcome the world."[10] Please don't kid yourself. There is no peace on earth until Jesus destroys the devil, the anti-Christ and the Beast and hurls them into the lake of fire.[11]

The remainder of that passage makes it clear Jesus calls us to love him more than any other thing or any other person. Surrendering your life for Jesus' sake is the only way to truly find life.

Again, speaking about the coming of the Kingdom of God, and after He predicted Peter's denial, Jesus said:

But now if you have a purse, take it, and also a bag; and
if you don't have a <u>sword</u>, sell your cloak and buy
one. It is written: 'And he was numbered with the
transgressors'; and I tell you that this must be fulfilled
in me. Yes, what is written about me is reaching its
fulfillment. The disciples said, "See, Lord, here are
two <u>swords</u>." "That's enough!" he replied.

— LUKE 22:36-38 (NIV)

Is it actually a physical sword? No. It is:

The <u>sword</u> of the Spirit, which is the <u>Word of God</u>.

— EPHESIANS 6:17 (NIV)

In fact, when one of the disciples used his *physical sword*
to cut off the ear of one of the great multitude who
came to arrest Jesus in Gethsemane, Jesus said to him:

<u>Put your sword in its place</u>, for all who <u>take by the sword</u>
<u>will perish by the sword</u>. Or do you think that I
cannot now pray to My Father, and He will provide
me with more than 12 legions of angels? How then
could the scriptures be fulfilled, that it must happen
thus?

— MATTHEW 26:51-54

Old Testament wars were manifested in the flesh. The New Covenant compels warfare in the Spirit. Hebrews explains it further:

> *For the Word of God is living and active, <u>sharper</u> than any <u>double-edged sword</u>, it penetrates even to dividing soul and spirit, joints and marrow; it judges the thoughts and attitudes of the heart. Nothing in all creation is hidden from God's sight. Everything is uncovered and laid bare before the eyes of him to whom we must give account.*

— HEBREWS 4:12-13 (NIV)

Isaiah prophesied:

> *He shall strike the earth with the rod of His mouth. And with the breath of His lips, He shall slay the wicked.*

— ISAIAH 11:4

To know Jesus' authentic toughness means we need to *buy* the Sword and use the Sword. The Sword is only the Word of God. These passages from the Word of God compel us to not just *read the Word*, but get the Word in us. Don't just get *in the Word*. We are called to get the *Word in us*. Once the Word is *in us*, *get it out*. Proclaim it. Confess it. Knowing Jesus means we have his Word in our spirit so that we can confess it in every circumstance; to witness to the lost; provide guidance in every tribulation we endure; and to attack wickedness through prayer and standing firm, never compromising. Jesus' Sword is all that can save us. There is nothing soft about Jesus' Sword.

DESTROYER

Jesus' authentic toughness compels us to understand Jesus is the **Destroyer**.[12] Why did Jesus come to earth?

> *The reason the Son of God appeared was to <u>destroy</u> the devil's work.*
>
> — 1 JOHN 3:8 (NIV)

Jesus' description of the coming of the Kingdom of God quoted above connects his Fire to Destruction.[13] In describing the last days when the Man of lawlessness appears, Paul writes:

> *And then the lawless one will be revealed, whom the Lord Jesus will overthrow with the <u>breath of his mouth</u> and <u>destroy</u> by the splendor of his coming.*
>
> — 2 THESSALONIANS 2:8 (NIV)

When addressing in detail the resurrection of Jesus, Paul wrote:

> *For as in Adam all die, even so in Christ all will be made alive. But each in his own turn: Christ, the first fruits; then, when He comes, those who belong to*

> *Him. Then the end will come, when He hands over*
> *the Kingdom to God the Father after He has <u>destroyed</u>*
> *<u>all dominion, authority and power</u>. For He must reign*
> *until He has put all His enemies under His feet.*

— 1 CORINTHIANS 15:22-26 (NIV)

Jesus' entire purpose was to destroy the work of the devil. Jesus will destroy all dominion, power and authority perpetrating evil and wickedness on the earth. There is nothing soft about Jesus, the Destroyer.

LIBERATOR

Knowing Jesus' authentic toughness compels us to understand Jesus is the **Liberator**.

Immediately after Jesus crushed all of Satan's temptations by using His Sword and speaking the Word of God to Satan (who had no choice but to flee), Jesus returned in the power of the Spirit to Galilee. He taught in multiple synagogues, being glorified by everyone. He came to Nazareth, where He was raised, went into the synagogue on the Sabbath Day and read Isaiah's prophesy *about Him*:

> *The Spirit of the Lord is upon me, because He has*
> *anointed Me to preach the gospel to the poor; He has*
> *sent me to heal the brokenhearted, to <u>proclaim liberty</u>*
> *<u>to the captives</u> and recovery of sight to the blind, to <u>set</u>*

> *at liberty those who are oppressed; to proclaim the*
> *acceptable year of the Lord.*
>
> — LUKE 4:18-19

John records Jesus' message to the Jews who believed Him:

> *If you abide in My Word, you are My disciples indeed.*
> *And you shall know the <u>truth</u>, and the <u>truth shall</u>*
> *<u>make you free</u>. They answered Him, "We are Abra-*
> *ham's descendants, and have never been in bondage to*
> *anyone. How can You say, 'You will be made free'?"*
> *Jesus answered them, "Most assuredly, I say to you,*
> *whoever commits sin is a slave of sin. And a slave*
> *does not abide in the house forever, but a son abides*
> *forever. Therefore, <u>if the Son makes you free, you shall</u>*
> *<u>be free indeed</u>."*
>
> — JOHN 8:31-36

Romans confirms there is no condemnation to those who are *in Jesus,* who do not walk according to the flesh, but according to the Spirit:

For the law of the Spirit of life in Christ Jesus has <u>made</u>
<u>me free</u> from the law of sin and death.
Because the creation itself will also be delivered from the
bondage of corruption into the <u>glorious liberty</u> of the
children of God.

— ROMANS 8:2, 21

Paul further writes:

Stand fast therefore in the <u>liberty</u> by which Christ has
<u>made us free</u>, and do not be entangled again with the
yoke of bondage.
For you, brethren, have been <u>called to liberty</u>; only do not
use liberty as an opportunity for the flesh, but through
love serve one another.

— GALATIANS 5:1, 13

When dealing with a woman who had a spirit of infirmity for 18 years, and who was bent over and could not
stand up, Jesus called her to Him and said to her:

Woman, you are <u>loosed</u> from your infirmity. And He laid
His hands on her, and immediately she was made
straight, and glorified God.

— LUKE 13:12-13

Surrendering all parts of our lives, repenting, and having great Faith in Jesus liberates and frees us from oppression, captivity, bondage and every type of sin. We are called to manifest our liberty not in the flesh, but in the Spirit. There is nothing soft about Jesus' status as the ultimate Liberator.

DIVIDER

Knowing Jesus' authentic toughness compels us to understand Jesus is a **Divider**. Immediately after the initial Fire on the earth statement quoted above, Jesus said:

> *Do you suppose that I came to give peace on earth? I tell you, not at all, but rather division.*

> — LUKE 12:51

Jesus' statement eviscerates the soft notion that He came to bring peace on earth. He certainly came to bring peace and goodwill to men and women *who believe*, but He absolutely came to split and divide faith from unbelief and wickedness. There is nothing soft about Jesus' status as a Divider.

CRUSHER

Knowing Jesus' authentic toughness compels us to understand Jesus is the **Crusher**. In the parable of the wicked vinedressers, Jesus stated:

> *Therefore I say to you, the Kingdom of God will be taken*
> *from you and given to a nation bearing the fruits of*
> *it. And whoever falls on this stone will be broken; but*
> *on whomever it falls, it will <u>grind him to powder</u>.*

— MATTHEW 21:43-44

Jesus confirmed His manifestation of the prophesy in Psalm 118:22-23 as the stone which the builders rejected which has become the chief cornerstone. Those responsible for killing prophets and the Son of God himself — which is every person who rejects Jesus — will be crushed by the capstone. There is nothing soft about Jesus' status as a Crusher.

PUNISHER

Knowing Jesus' authentic toughness compels us to understand Jesus is the **Punisher**. When confronting the hypocrisy and oppressive nature of the scribes and teachers of the law, Jesus said:

While all the people were listening, Jesus said to his disciples, "Beware of the teachers of the law. They like to walk around in flowing robes and love to be greeted with respect in the marketplaces and have the most important seats in the synagogues and the places of honor at banquets. They devour widows' houses and for a show make lengthy prayers. These men will be <u>punished most severely</u>."

— LUKE 20:45-47; SEE ALSO, MARK 12:38-40 (NIV)

Paul also addresses this:

All this is evidence that God's judgment is right, and as a result you will be counted worthy of the kingdom of God, for which you are suffering. God is just: He will pay back trouble to those who trouble you and give relief to you who are troubled, and to us as well. This will happen when the <u>Lord Jesus is revealed from heaven in blazing fire</u> with his powerful angels. He will <u>punish those who do not know God and do not obey the gospel of our Lord Jesus</u>.

— 2 THESSALONIANS 1:5-10 (NIV)

Any unrepentant person who imposes oppression, tyranny and tribulation on people of Faith will be punished. There is nothing soft about Jesus' status as the Punisher.

37

SILENCER

Knowing Jesus' authentic toughness compels us to understand Jesus is the **Silencer**. After healing a man with palsy on the Sabbath, Jesus spoke to the lawyers and Pharisees, saying:

> *"Is it lawful to heal on the Sabbath?" But they kept silent. And He took him and healed him, and let him go. Then He answered them, saying, "Which of you, having a donkey or an ox that has fallen into a pit, will not immediately pull him out on the Sabbath day?" And they could not answer Him regarding these things.*
>
> — LUKE 14:3-6

Addressing the Pharisees' attempt to trap Jesus whether it was lawful to pay taxes to Caesar and demanding receipt of a denarius, Jesus famously stated, "Render therefore to Caesar the things that are Caesar's, and to God the things that are God's." Luke records:

> *But they could not catch Him in His words in the presence of the people. And they marveled at His answer and kept silent.*
>
> — LUKE 20:26

Addressing the Sadducees' unbelief in the resurrection, Jesus confirmed that people were neither married nor be given in marriage in the age to come, in response to a complex series of questions and seemingly logical traps. Jesus summarized the Word of God and concluded:

> *"For He is not the God of the dead but of the living, for all live to Him." Then some of the scribes answered and said, "Teacher, You, have spoken well." But after that they <u>dared not question Him anymore</u>.*

> — LUKE 20:38-39

When confronted with potential inconsistencies in the Word, and logical traps attempted to be set, answer simply with the Word using the Sword of the Spirit and the fools will be silenced. There is nothing soft about Jesus the Silencer.

HUMILIATOR

Knowing Jesus' authentic toughness compels us to understand Jesus had no trouble being the **Humiliator**. After liberating the woman with the spirit of infirmity quoted above, the ruler of the synagogue answered Jesus with indignation about healing on the Sabbath. The Lord answered him and said:

> *"Hypocrite! Does not each one of you on the Sabbath loose his ox or donkey from the stall, and lead it away to water it? So ought not this woman, being a daughter of Abraham, whom <u>Satan has bound</u>—think of it—for eighteen years, be <u>loosed</u> from this*

> *bond on the Sabbath?" When he said this, all his*
> *opponents were <u>humiliated</u>, but the people were*
> *<u>delighted</u> with all the wonderful things he was doing.*

— LUKE 13:15-16, LUKE 13:17(NIV)

Jesus crushed both the spirit of infirmity and the spirit of religion all in the same discussion. His adversaries were put to shame. Jesus addressed oppression, lack of faith and indignation for not following oppressive rules with the Word. In these limited circumstances, when any person twists the Word of God, there is no sin in effectuating humiliation and shame against unbelief. There is nothing soft about Jesus the Humiliator.

INFURIATOR

Knowing Jesus' authentic toughness compels us to understand Jesus is the **Infuriator.** Following Jesus' proclamation that He would bring liberty to the captives and the oppressed, He announced Isaiah's prophesy was fulfilled in front of those people.[14] Jesus then quoted additional prophesies, the faith implemented by Elijah and the double portion of blessing bestowed on Elisha. Luke records their response:

> *All the people in the synagogue were <u>furious</u> when they*
> *heard this. They got up, drove him out of the town,*
> *and took him to the brow of the hill on which the*
> *town was built, in order to throw him off the cliff.*

But he walked right through the crowd and went on his way.

— LUKE 4:28-30 (NIV)

Speaking a prophetic word and using the Sword of the Spirit, which is the Word, will infuriate oppressors, deniers and opponents of Jesus. They may be filled with wrath and get furious when the Word is spoken in the Spirit. There is nothing soft about Jesus the Infuriator.

OFFENDER

Knowing Jesus' authentic toughness compels us to understand Jesus is the **Offender**. Jesus addressed the scribes and the Pharisees who challenged Jesus about the disciples transgressing the tradition of the elders because they did not wash their hands when they ate bread. Jesus reasserted the commandments and multiple Old Testament references and prophesies, ultimately concluding that defilement is not external, but internal. He said to them:

> *"Hear and understand: Not what goes into the mouth defiles a man; but what comes out of the mouth, this defiles a man." Then His disciples came and said to Him, "Do You know that the Pharisees were offended when they heard this saying?" But He answered and said, "Every plant which My heavenly Father has not planted will be uprooted. Let them alone. They*

> are <u>blind leaders of the blind</u>. And if the <u>blind leads the blind</u>, both will fall into a ditch."
>
> — MATTHEW 15:10-14

Respond to any distortion of the Word and the Truth with the Sword of the Spirit, which is the actual Word of God. Be direct. Be accurate. People may be offended. If the recipient of the Word is offended, that is not your problem. After teaching many people many parables, Jesus went home, taught in the synagogue, and the people were astonished with respect to Jesus' wisdom and His mighty works. Matthew records:

> Is this not the carpenter's son? Is not His mother called Mary? And His brothers James, Joseph, Simon and Judas? And His sisters, are they not all with us? Where did this Man get all these things? So they were <u>offended</u> at Him. But Jesus said to them, "A prophet is not without honor except in his own country and in his own house." Now he did not do many mighty works there because of their <u>unbelief</u>.
>
> — MATTHEW 13:55-58

The absolute authority of Jesus' wisdom, truth and healing will be offensive. Do not expect any mighty work in your life if you walk in unbelief or are offended at Jesus. There is nothing soft about Jesus the Offender.

INSULTER

Knowing Jesus' authentic toughness compels us to understand Jesus is the **Insulter**. Luke records another circumstance in which a Pharisee ate dinner with Jesus. The Pharisee raised a concern that Jesus did not first wash before eating dinner. Jesus then launched into a series of attacks beginning with the phrase "woe to you Pharisees!" One of the experts of the law answered Jesus:

> *"Teacher, when you say these things, you **insult** us also." Jesus replied, "And you experts in the law, woe to you, because you load people down with burdens they can hardly carry, and you yourselves will not lift one finger to help them."*

> — LUKE 11:45-46 (NIV)

Jesus literally slammed the Pharisees three times. The legal experts objected because they were insulted. In Matthew 11:46-52, Jesus followed with three more attacks. These people were exalting religion and restriction over faith, freedom, justice and love. The call is to speak the Word in Truth and Love. If the recipient is insulted along the way, that is no sin. There is nothing soft about Jesus the Insulter.

CORRECTOR

Jesus' authentic toughness compels us to understand that Jesus is the **Corrector**. In squarely addressing the Sadducees' disavowment of the resurrection, Jesus said to them:

> *"Are you not therefore <u>mistaken</u>, because you do not know the scriptures nor the power of God? For when they rise from the dead, they neither marry nor are given in marriage, but are like angels in heaven. But concerning the dead, that they rise, have you not read in the Book of Moses, in the burning bush passage, how God spoke to him, saying 'I am the God of Abraham, the God of Isaac and the God of Jacob?' He is not the God of the dead, but the God of the living. You are therefore <u>greatly mistaken</u>."*
>
> — MARK 12:24-27

Jesus deals with rejection of every one of God's principles by quoting the Word. Every mistaken view with which you are confronted compels a singularly focused response based on the Word of God. There is nothing soft about Jesus the Corrector.

BOUNCER

Jesus' authentic toughness compels us to understand that Jesus is the **Bouncer**.

Jesus entered the temple courts and drove out all who were buying and selling there. He <u>overturned the tables</u> of the money changers and the benches of those selling doves. "It is written," he said to them, "'My house will be called a house of prayer,' but you are making it 'a den of robbers.'"

— MATTHEW 21:12-13 (NIV)

When it was almost time for the Jewish Passover, Jesus went up to Jerusalem. In the temple courts he found men selling cattle, sheep and doves, and others sitting at tables exchanging money. So, he made a <u>whip out of cords</u>, and drove them all from the temple area, both sheep and cattle; he scattered the coins of the money changers and <u>overturned</u> their tables. To those who sold doves he said, "get these out of here! How dare you turn my Father's house into a market!" His disciples remembered that it is written: "Zeal for your house will consume me."

— JOHN 2:13-17 (NIV)

Jesus lacks any tolerance for distorting what must occur in the House of God, i.e., praise, worship, Word, encouragement and helping each other. There is nothing soft about Jesus the Bouncer.

REBUKER

Jesus' authentic toughness compels us to understand Jesus is the **Rebuker**. Following Jesus' resurrection, Mark records the following:

> *Later He appeared to the eleven as they sat at the table; and He <u>rebuked</u> their unbelief and hardness of heart, because they did not believe those who had seen Him after He had risen.*

> — MARK 16:14

This rebuke constituted a sharp disapproval and criticism against Jesus' actual followers. Jesus will rebuke lack of faith. Jesus will rebuke stubborn refusal to believe God. Jesus will rebuke stubborn refusal to believe testimony. When demonstrating lack of faith or stubborn refusal to believe God and other people's testimony, expect rebuke. It's a teaching tool that every Spiritual Warrior needs to receive at times. Remember:

> *They triumphed over him [the devil] by the <u>blood of the Lamb</u> and by the <u>word of their testimony</u>; they did not love their lives so much as to shrink from death.*

> — REVELATION 12:11

Give and receive testimony. Walk in faith. Believe God. Believe testimony. There is nothing soft about Jesus the Rebuker.

DISARMER

Jesus' authentic toughness compels us to understand Jesus is the **Disarmer**. In addressing the need for absolute faith and not legalism, Paul wrote:

> *And you, being dead in your trespasses and the uncircumcision of your flesh, He has made <u>alive together with Him</u>, having wiped out the handwriting of requirements that was against us, which was contrary to us. And He has taken it out of the way, having nailed it to the cross. Having <u>disarmed</u> principalities and powers, He made a public spectacle of them, triumphing over them in it.*

> — COLOSSIANS 2:13-15

Jesus' crucifixion was the toughest, most loving act in the history of the world. Walking in Faith means we are alive together with Him and in Him. Jesus obliterated all evil and wickedness on the cross. He made a public spectacle of the devil and triumphed over all sin and evil. There is nothing soft about Jesus the Disarmer.

EXCRUCIATOR

Jesus' authentic toughness compels us to understand Jesus is the **Excruciator**.[15] The word "excruciating" finds its origin in the Latin, meaning *tormented on a cross*. Artistic works tend to illustrate Jesus on the cross as

47

skinny, weak and defeated. On the contrary, It was the ultimate act of toughness, grit and love. Jesus endured excruciating, unendurable, racking and agonizing pain, anguish, suffering and torture immediately after his trial and throughout His crucifixion. Jesus *voluntarily* endured excruciating suffering for our sins. Jesus was sinless, but bore all of our sins out of love, with infinite grit.

Please read the Gospel accounts of Jesus' trial, beatings and crucifixion to completely identify with this level of toughness. Jesus was betrayed multiple times. His closest friends and followers denied him multiple times. Jesus was sorrowful and deeply distressed. Jesus said:

> *My soul is exceeding sorrowful, even to death. Stay here and watch with me.*
> *He fell on his face and prayed to God to let the excruciating agony pass from Him but immediately subjugated His own will to the Father's will.*

> — MATTHEW 26:38-39

Jesus was completely forsaken by His friends and closest followers.[16] On the cross he cried out in a loud voice asking God why the Heavenly Father had forsaken Him.[17]

Jesus endured a mockery of injustice, which included, by my account, more than a dozen different violations of constitutional and criminal legal procedural rights under current standards of United States law. Jesus was scourged. A scourge was a whip used as instrument of punishment. Some Bible scholars theorized that Jesus endured the maximum 39 lashings as determined by Jewish law, but no one knows for sure. The Roman soldiers may have ignored the law and whipped Him even more. His flesh was likely torn, and probably shredded so that part of His spine may have been exposed by the deep cuts. Jesus was mocked repeatedly.[18] The Roman soldiers jammed a twisted crown of thorns into his head.[19] They spit on Jesus, and struck him on the head, possibly driving the thorns further into his head, magnifying both His blood shed and His pain.[20]

Then they crucified Him. Nails were driven in Jesus' wrists and feet. Having endured an already unimaginable amount of pain through the whipping and beating, the nails driven into Jesus' wrists and feet with His arms stretched outward created the most agony possible. Jesus would have had to continually push against His feet to breathe, but breathing would send more pain through every nerve in His body. Then one of the soldiers pierced His side with a spear, resulting in immediate blood and water flow.[21]

We tend to gloss over the excruciating agony Jesus endured. Reading all four Gospel accounts of His trial, whipping, beating and crucifixion confirms what Jesus endured for our sins. All of Jesus' excruciating agony fulfilled the prophecy that He would be despised and rejected; be full of sorrow and grief; stricken; afflicted; wounded for our transgressions; bruised for our iniquities; chastised for our peace and reconciliation with the Lord God Almighty.[22] Remember this. Also remember that by His stripes we are healed.[23] There is nothing soft about Jesus' status as the Excruciator.

HATER

Jesus' authentic toughness compels us to understand Jesus, under extremely limited circumstances, is the **Hater**. In addressing the compromising church in Pergamos, Jesus said:

> *Thus, you also have those who hold the doctrine of the Nicolaitans, which thing I hate.*

> — REVELATION 2:15

Bible scholars debate exactly what this means, but the consensus appears to be that the Nicolaitans buckled under the pressures of Roman governmental rule, lost their faith, fell in love with idolatrous teaching, and seemed to want to drag other believers in Jesus down with them. Jesus tolerates none of this. There is nothing soft about Jesus the Hater of idolatry, abandoning faith and buckling to government-imposed idolatry.

ENFORCER

Jesus' authentic toughness compels us to understand Jesus is the **Enforcer**. Following the resurrection, Jesus came and spoke to His disciples, saying:

> *All authority has been given to Me in heaven and on*
> *earth. Go therefore and make disciples of all the*
> *nations, baptizing them in the name of the Father*
> *and of the Son and of the Holy Spirit, teaching them*
> *to observe all things that I have commanded you; and*
> *lo, I am with you always, even to the end of the age.*
>
> — MATTHEW 28:18-20

This means Jesus became the highest ranking officer in heaven. Jesus possesses absolute authority over the entire Word.[24] Jesus possesses absolute authority over every demon and unclean spirit.[25] Jesus possesses absolute authority over disease and all healing.[26] This means Jesus, as the New Covenant, enforces all of God's promises and covenants.

But that is not the end of it. Jesus has transferred His absolute authority to every person who walks in faith. Jesus said:

> *I saw Satan fall like lightning from heaven. Behold, I give*
> *you the authority to trample on serpents and scorpions,*
> *and over all of the power of the enemy, and nothing*
> *shall by any means hurt you.*
>
> — LUKE 10:18-19

What is the difference between "authority" and "power?" Revelation knowledge indicates the difference can be explained by the legal concept known as *jurisdiction*. A federal judge possesses enormous *power* to interpret the law. But *without jurisdiction* (based on a claim arising under a federal statute, regulation or the United States Constitution), the federal judge has zero authority. Jurisdiction derives from the Latin "say the law." The law is the entirety of the Word of God. Saying the law means Jesus has given every true believer who walks in Faith the ability to speak the Word over every circumstance in life. Authority is influence predicated on legitimacy. Power is an entity or individual's ability to control or direct others. Knowing Jesus' authentic toughness means we have legitimate influence over every circumstance, including all of the power that Satan may assert against us. Jesus will enforce the entirety of the Word. Jesus has given us all of that authority, and it is received following repentance, acknowledging Jesus as the Savior, and when the Holy Spirit comes upon us.[27] There is nothing soft about Jesus the Enforcer.

CLOSER

Jesus' authentic toughness compels us to understand Jesus is the **Closer**. In baseball, the manager calls in the "closer" to *save the game*. Hebrews states:

> *Looking unto Jesus, the author and <u>finisher</u> of our faith, who for the joy that was set before Him endured the cross, despising the shame, and has <u>sat down at the right hand of the throne of God</u>.*

> — HEBREWS 12:2

As demonstrated by the quotes from Revelation outlined above, at the appointed time, the Lord God Almighty will call in the Right Hander and close out the battle on the earth. There is nothing soft about Jesus the Closer.

VICTOR

Jesus authentic toughness compels us to understand that Jesus is the **Victor**. John writes:

> For everyone born of God *overcomes* the world. This is the *victory* that has overcome the world, even our *faith*. Who is it that overcomes the world? Only the one who *believes that Jesus is the Son of God*.

> — 1 JOHN 5:4-5 (NIV)

There is nothing soft about Jesus the ultimate Victor.

The authentic Jesus is the perfect manifestation of God.[28] Jesus is the express image of God. Jesus is both the Lion of Judah and the Lamb of God. Jesus is truth and love. He is justice and mercy. He brings judgment but provides grace. He compels us to walk by faith, not by fear.

---

1. 1 John 2:6.
2. Tolerance is defined by the world to require Christians to accept the world's view of life and sin. Exhibiting remarkable intellectual dishonesty, the world refuses to tolerate Jesus' world view and disdain for sin. The truth is Jesus loves everyone and died for everyone. But he will not tolerate wickedness.

3. Revelation 19:11-16 (NIV).
4. Revelation 20:9 (NIV).
5. *What is Fire? See,* ScienceLearn.org.nz.
6. *Id.*
7. Revelation 20:13 (NIV).
8. Revelation 1:16 (NIV).
9. Luke 2:14.
10. John 16:33.
11. Revelation 20:13-14.
12. Jesus came to destroy sin and the devil's work. This is not to be confused with the destroyer referenced in Revelation 9:11, which references a bottomless pit, often appearing alongside the place of Sheol, meaning the resting place of dead people.
13. Luke 17:27-28.
14. Luke 4:21 (NIV).
15. The word "excruciating" is an adjective. "Excruciator" is a newly created noun so we can identify exactly what Jesus endured for our sins.
16. Matthew 26:56.
17. Matthew 27:46.
18. Matthew 27:29,39-44.
19. Matthew 27:29.
20. Matthew 27:30-31.
21. John 19:34.
22. Isaiah 53:3-5.
23. Isaiah 53:5.
24. Mark 1:22.
25. Mark 1:27.
26. Mark 1:34; Mark 3:15.
27. Acts 1:8.
28. Hebrews 1:3 (NIV).

CHAPTER 3
JESUS' LOVE AND TRUTH

The most famous, often quoted passage upon which the entire Gospel rests is revealed in Jesus' words to Nicodemus:

> *For God so <u>loved</u> the world, that He gave His only*
> *begotten Son, that whoever believes in Him should not*
> *perish but have everlasting life. For God did not send*
> *His Son into the world to condemn the world, but*
> *that the world through Him might be saved.*

> —JOHN 3:16-17

Jesus' love for every person – the saved, the lost and even the wicked – is sacrificial. It is not static or self-centered. Jesus' love is designed to reach out and draw others to Him. Jesus set the pattern of true love, which is the basis for all love relationships. When you love someone dearly, you will pay dearly for that person's responsive love. God paid dearly with the life of His Son, Jesus, the highest price He could pay. Jesus accepted our punishment, paid the price for our sins, and then offers us new life that He has purchased for us.

In Jesus' proverbial locker room speech to His disciples immediately preceding His crucifixion, Jesus said:

> _Greater love_ has no one than this, then to lay down one's
> life for his friends.
>
> —JOHN 15:13

Paul explained Jesus' love like this:

> _Yet in all these things we are more than conquerors through
> Him who loved us. For I am persuaded that neither
> death nor life, nor angels nor principalities nor
> powers, nor things present nor things to come, nor
> height nor depth, nor any other created thing, shall be
> able to separate us from the love of God which is in
> Christ Jesus our Lord._
>
> — ROMANS 8:37-39

Jesus' love is beyond measure. Jesus' love for people is profound. No matter what happens, no matter what life's circumstances may be, we can never be lost to Jesus' love. Jesus' love is eternal. Jesus' love is unconquerable. People who walk in faith in Jesus possess absolute security in Him.

Much more has been and can be written about Jesus'

immeasurable love. This aspect of Jesus' essential being is ubiquitous and permeates everything.

Jesus' Truth, as quoted above in the context of his exclusivity, is revealed in His answer to Thomas' inquiry suggesting the disciples did not know where he was going and how they can know the way. Jesus said:

> *I am the way, the <u>truth</u> and the life. No one comes to the Father except through Me.*
>
> —JOHN 14:6

Jesus' enormous sacrificial Love is balanced with his absolute Truth. Jesus' Truth is manifested through the entirety of His Word. Facts can be accurate, but Jesus *is the absolute Truth.* Jesus' Truth and the freedom that follows is conditional. Jesus said to the Jews who believed Him:

> *If you <u>abide in My Word</u>, you are My disciples, indeed. And you shall <u>know the truth</u> and the <u>truth shall make you free</u>.*
> *Therefore, if the <u>Son makes you free, you shall be free indeed</u>.*
>
> —JOHN 8:31-32, 36

Jesus is the absolute source of truth. Jesus is the perfect standard of what is right. Jesus frees us from the consequences of sin, self-deception and deception by Satan.

Simply because we *know facts* does not mean we know truth and we are free. The conditions precedent quoted above require us to literally live every aspect of our lives in His Word. *Then* we are certainly His disciples. *Only then* can we know the truth and be free.

CHAPTER 4
PRACTICAL APPLICATION OF JESUS'
PERFECT LOVE, TRUTH AND FIRE

K nowing Jesus' authentic toughness through Jesus' Fire combined with Jesus' perfect Truth and perfect Love allows us to live in Him. We achieve this only when we are led by the Spirit and not by our flesh. We then have standing to receive benefits and blessings. We then, and only then, have legal standing to boldly approach the Throne of Grace and obtain Mercy.[1]

To the misinformed people who think Jesus was (or is) soft, you now understand His authentic toughness, perfect Love, perfect Truth and perfect Fire.

To lost people who live in unbelief, there is no other path to eternal life except through Jesus' perfect Love and perfect Truth.

To people who reject and blaspheme Jesus, and manifest wickedness in the earth, please understand it will not end well for you. This is another chance to connect with the perfect Savior.

To people who are incarcerated legally or figuratively because of bondage, Jesus' perfect love, perfect Truth and perfect Fire; your repentance; and your decision to walk with Jesus in His Word will absolutely set you free.

To pastors and priests who propagate a soft Jesus to justify weakness, unbelief, lack of faith or to advance either extreme of a political agenda in contradiction of God's unequivocal Word, stop it. Stop it now. Stop playing church. Stop worrying about your job. Stop concerning yourself with curtains, carpets, the budget, the Board of Directors, your pension and any external distractions. Get over yourself. Do everything you can, short of sinning, to bring lost people to faith in Jesus and preach Jesus' authentic toughness.

To Spiritual Warriors walking in great faith who tend to rely on Jesus' authentic toughness solely in the flesh and not in the spirit, we, likewise, must repent and be led by the Spirit. We can certainly hate evil and wickedness and the seven things God detests.[2] We stand our ground against wickedness and do not shrink back. But to be just, we must live by pure Faith.[3] We must love the person while attacking the wickedness in spiritual warfare:

If anyone says, "I love God," yet hates his brother, he is a liar. For anyone who does <u>not love his brother</u>, whom he has seen, cannot love God, whom he has not seen. And he has given us this command: Whoever <u>loves God must also love his brother</u>.

— 1 JOHN 4:20-21 (NIV)

Spiritual Warriors are particularly compelled to bring Jesus' Fire critically tempered by "<u>speaking truth in love</u>."[4]

Knowing Jesus' authentic toughness and living His perfect Love and Truth has additional blessings in this life as well as eternal life. We walk in Jesus' power and authority. We receive blessings, grace, mercy and every gift that He has for us. We overcome everything and every stronghold in every aspect of life that the enemy has intended to steal, kill or destroy. We are more than conquerors. We are Sons of God.

Knowing Jesus' authentic toughness in combination with His perfect Love and perfect Truth exemplifies the true nature of God and establishes the exclusive basis of Faith.

This is written so that you may believe that Jesus is the Christ, the Son of God, and that believing you may have life in His Holy Name.[5]

---

1. Hebrews 4:16.
2. Romans 12:9; Hebrews 1:9; Psalm 45:7; and Proverbs 6:16-19.

3. Hebrews 10:38-39.
4. Ephesians 4:15 (NIV).
5. John 20:31 (NIV).

About the Author

Charlie Artz has practiced healthcare law for 34 years in Harrisburg, Pennsylvania. He has briefed and argued more than two dozen cases in Pennsylvania appellate courts and the United States Court of Appeals and won a case in the Pennsylvania Supreme Court. His writing style is characterized by compelling advocacy, linear logic, simplification of complex issues, and humor. Teaching is his primary spiritual gift. Coupled with his legal skills, his gifting provides a unique platform to proclaim the Gospel of Jesus Christ. Charlie unabashedly shares his Faith and encourages others to do so. He has been called to recruit, equip, train, and mobilize spiritual warriors for spiritual battle in the marketplace, the gym, the home, and the ballpark to facilitate a personal move of God in people's lives for transformation and revival. He operates in Faith without fear. He is blessed to be the dad of four beautiful, brilliant, and redeemed children.

Contact Charlie here: info@riseuppublications.com